An Insider's Guide to
SOCCER

JEREMY COOPERSON AND BRIAN WINGATE

rosen publishing's
rosen central

NEW YORK

Published in 2015 by The Rosen Publishing Group, Inc.
29 East 21st Street, New York, NY 10010

First Edition

Library of Congress Cataloging-in-Publication Data

Cooperson, Jeremy.
An insider's guide to soccer/Jeremy Cooperson and Brian Wingate.
    pages cm.—(Sports tips, techniques, and strategies)
Includes bibliographical references and index.
ISBN 978-1-4777-8591-1 (library bound)—ISBN 978-1-4777-8592-8 (pbk.)—
ISBN 978-1-4777-8594-2 (6-pack)
1. Soccer. I. Wingate, Brian. II. Title.
GV943.C586 2015
796.334—dc23

                                                                        2013043288

Manufactured in the United States of America

Metric Conversion Chart			
1 inch	2.54 centimeters 25.4 millimeters	1 cup	250 milliliters
1 foot	30.48 centimeters	1 ounce	28 grams
1 yard	.914 meters	1 fluid ounce	30 milliliters
1 square foot	.093 square meters	1 teaspoon	5 milliliters
1 square mile	2.59 square kilometers	1 tablespoon	15 milliliters
1 ton	.907 metric tons	1 quart	.946 liters
1 pound	454 grams	355 degrees F	180 degrees C
1 mile	1.609 kilometers		

Contents

CHAPTER 1 4

The History of Soccer

CHAPTER 2 12

The Field and Players

CHAPTER 3 24

Playing the Game

CHAPTER 4 36

Getting Involved

GLOSSARY 42

FOR MORE INFORMATION 43

FOR FURTHER READING 45

BIBLIOGRAPHY 46

INDEX 47

The History of Soccer

There are accounts throughout history from all over the world of people playing games in which they moved a ball across a playing field toward a goal at the other end. In Mexico, the Maya played their own version of a kicking game, called Pok-A-Tok, as early as 3000 BCE. Archaeologists have unearthed a playing field that is more than 3,500 years old! Historical records also show that the Chinese played a game similar to soccer for their emperor's birthday celebration in about 2500 BCE. They called the game Tsu Chu, meaning "to kick a stuffed leather ball."

In Croatia, the second-century tombstone of a seven-year-old boy, Gaius Laberius, shows him holding a ball with hexagons joined in the manner of a net–like ornament.

Around 2000 BCE, the Greeks played a game called Episkyros with a ball made from inflated pig bladders. Earlier models were constructed of linen and hair wrapped tightly in string and then sewn together. The Romans created their own version of the game, Harpastum, which used a smaller ball and was played more like rugby than soccer.

Mob Football

In the eighth century, people in Britain took part in mob football, in which entire villages played against each other. These matches were so violent that many hid in their homes and shuttered the windows. The origins of mob football are unclear, but one story speaks of the severed head of a defeated prince being used as the ball.

Over the centuries, attempts were made to reduce the sport's violent side. Britain's King Edward II was so disturbed that he banned mob football in 1314. The ban did not work and for the next four hundred years, several European rulers attempted to stop their subjects from playing the sport. In France, Kings Philippe V and Charles V both tried to outlaw the violent game. During the fifteenth century, Scottish kings James I and James II tried to keep football out of their country. In 1540, King Henry VIII of England outlawed football, even though there is evidence that he played the sport himself. Finally, in 1681, football gained royal approval when King Charles II of England publicly attended a match.

Making the Rules

In 1815, Eton College in England established a set of rules that other teams began to follow. In 1848, these rules were officially adopted and named the Cambridge Rules. This marked a crossroads for the sport, which was called football at the time. Players in Britain soon divided into two camps. One side supported the Cambridge Rules and the attempt to reduce violence in the sport. (Under the new rules, tripping and "hacking," or shin kicking, were prohibited.) Other players preferred to follow the rules set by the Rugby School, which were considerably rougher.

An artist's depiction of a school football game in Britain, 1887.

To settle the dispute, the sport was split in two by the London Football Association in 1863. There was rugby football, which kept many of the old rules. Then there was association football, which became soccer as we know it today.

Refining the rules fueled the popularity of soccer in Britain. Amateur soccer clubs sprouted up everywhere, and the first annual tournament was established in 1871. The following year, England and Scotland met in the first international match.

Football or Soccer?

The term "soccer" came about in the 1880s at Oxford University, in Great Britain. A slang term for rugby was "rugger." A player named Charles Wreford Brown took the middle of the word "association" football, added an "er," and coined the term "soccer." In North America, the term stuck. However, most fans around the world (including those in Britain) still refer to their beloved sport as football.

The Formation of FIFA

Soccer spread around the globe, and it soon became clear that there was a need for international rules. In 1904, seven European soccer associations founded the Fédération Internationale de Football Association, or FIFA. FIFA was designed to oversee soccer operations throughout the world and encourage a high level of competition.

FIFA certainly achieved its goals. In 1930, the first World Cup tournament was held in Uruguay, South America, to determine the best team in soccer. Uruguay took advantage of the home field and won the World Cup that year. The United States stood third in the tournament, a position the nation has been unable to better since then. Since 1930, the popularity of the World Cup has only grown. In 2013, FIFA boasted of more member countries (209) than the United Nations. The level of competition for the World Cup championship is fierce, and passions run high. The tournament is now held every four years, with the top thirty-two teams of the world competing for the Cup.

Poster publicizing FIFA's first World Cup, held in 1930.

Women's Soccer Enters the Picture

The 1990s were an eventful year for American women soccer players. First, in 1991, the U.S. women's team won the FIFA World Cup tournament held in China. It was the first World Cup championship for any American team. Four years later, they made another strong World Cup showing, coming in third in the tournament held in Sweden. When the United States hosted the 1999 World Cup, more than three million

Mia Hamm (in white) was in large part responsible for popularizing the sport among women. Here, she is shown playing against Germany in 1997.

fans attended the tournament games. Millions more worldwide watched the action on television. Led by Mia Hamm, the American women's team bagged the World Cup, after beating the Chinese women's team in a shoot-out.

Women's soccer began to gain popularity all over the world in the 1990s. Here, USA plays against Japan in the 2012 Summer Olympics in London.

Pelé Visits America

A major contribution to soccer's growth in the United States was a visit from a huge Brazilian star with a short name: Pelé. Born Edson Arantes do Nascimento, Pelé is considered by many to be the best player in the history of the sport. He became a worldwide star when he led Brazil to three World Cup trophies from 1958 to 1970. He retired in 1974.

At the time of his retirement, professional soccer had been struggling to find an audience in North America. Then, in 1975, the New York Cosmos of the North American Soccer League (NASL) persuaded Pelé to come out of retirement and play for them. Electrifying audiences for another three years, Pelé and his presence on the American soccer scene put the sport in the spotlight. Thousands of kids across the United States picked up soccer, which was easy and fun to play and required little equipment. Though the NASL shut in 1984, another NASL (unaffiliated to the first) was founded in 2009. It currently plays with eight teams in the U.S. and Canada.

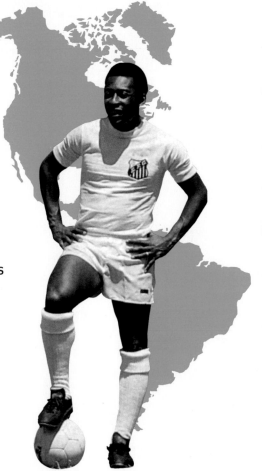

Pelé, born on 21st October 1940, is regarded by experts, critics, and fans as the best player in the history of the sport.

A New Age

Major League Soccer (MLS) was established in 1996 by the United States Soccer Federation in exchange for hosting the men's World Cup in 1994. Nearly 20 years later, Major League Soccer is well established, although it has not yet generated the same level of fan support as basketball, football, and baseball in the United States. Hockey, Canada's national sport, still dominates the headlines up north. But youth leagues are popular all over North America, and every year the number of people who enjoy this sport keeps increasing.

An MLS game between the Vancouver Whitecaps (in white) and the Los Angeles Chivas highlights the growing popularity of soccer in Canada.

CHAPTER 2

The Field and Players

The United States Soccer Federation has pegged the total number of Americans who play soccer at over twenty-four million. And the number is on the rise. According to an article published in the *New York Times,* the number of high school soccer players more than doubled between 1990 and 2010, giving soccer the fastest growth rate among all major U.S. sports. Many schools have their own soccer fields, where students play during the week. On the weekends, these same fields often play host to popular local league games.

What's The Goal?

A rectangular goal, usually a frame made of metal, sits in the middle of each goal line. Goal posts and crossbars must be white. A regulation goal is eight feet tall and eight yards wide. A net is attached to the frame to catch any balls that get past the goalkeeper, or goalie, the player who guards the goal. The net is about six feet in depth.

Though the goal is quite large in comparison to the ball, scoring is not as easy as it might seem.

Where's it Played?

Generally, short-cut grass covers the entire surface of a soccer field—also called a pitch. The field may vary in size, depending on the league, but it must be a rectangle. The two halves of the field are separated by the center line. In the middle of this line is a circle with a 10-yard radius. The ball is placed in the center of this circle at the beginning of both halves of the match and after goals, to restart play.

The area in front of the goal is marked with two rectangles. The smaller one is the goal area, and the larger one is the penalty area. The goalie (and only the goalie) may handle the ball (that is, use his or her hands) in the penalty area.

A flag marks each corner of a soccer field. A quarter-circle is drawn within the field, one yard from the flag post. Corner kicks are special kicks made with the ball placed in these quarter-circles.

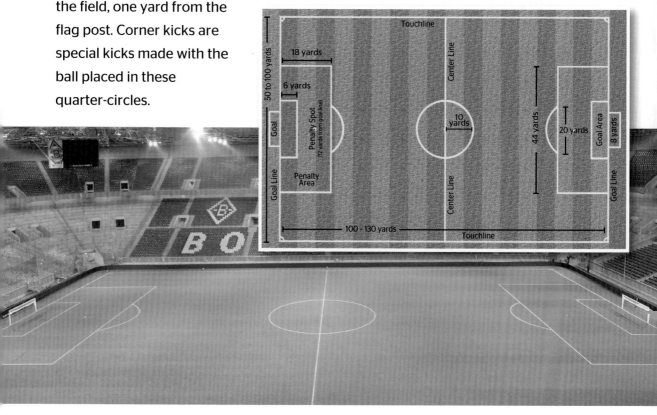

Although the size of the field may differ depending on the league, in order to be approved by the FIFA for international games, a field must be between 100 and 130 yards long and 50 to 100 yards wide.

What's it Played With?

The ball used by most leagues is made of leather or other FIFA-approved materials. Balls come in several sizes. Upper levels use a ball that is approximately 27 to 28 inches in circumference and weighs about one pound. Youth leagues often use a smaller, lighter ball.

Who Plays?

The maximum number of players on a team varies depending on the level. Professional teams usually have a total of about fourteen players. At game time, each team has eleven players on the field. The rest wait until one of their teammates needs a break. World Cup rules allow a maximum of three substitutions per match, so team sizes are kept relatively small. Youth leagues with unlimited substitution may have over twenty players.

The English team Chelsea FC poses for a photo after winning the UEFA Champions League Final game at Allianz Arena on May 19, 2012 in Munich, Germany.

What are the Positions?

There are some basic player positions that every team uses. Each player has a certain zone or area of the field that he or she patrols.

Goalie

In some ways the goalie is the most important player on the field. It's the goalie's job to protect the goal and keep the other team from scoring. The goalie (also called a goalkeeper or keeper) can use any part of the body to protect the goal while he or she is in the penalty

Only goalies can use their hands to try and stop a ball from entering the goal.

box area. A good goalkeeper is calm under pressure and is not afraid to jump in the way of a speeding ball. As an attacking player approaches with the ball, the keeper stands in a slight crouch, ready to spring in any direction. The keeper may suddenly charge toward the oncoming player, reducing the chance for a good shot on goal. During a corner kick, the keeper will often lunge into the air and knock the ball away with a closed fist. The ability to use his or her hands helps the goalie rise above the crowd and reach the ball first. Once out of the penalty area, however, the keeper is treated like any other player and may not use his or her hands. This is why goalies prefer to remain within the penalty area, unless the ball is deep in the opponent's area.

Defenders

Three or four players usually patrol the area around their goal to defend the team from attackers. Center-backs and fullbacks serve as the goalkeeper's last line of protection. When the opposing team tries to score, these backs try to take the ball away by disrupting the play.

The defender (in yellow and black) is trying to stop the attacker of the opposing team from dribbling the ball ahead and scoring.

Most teams use four defensive players and employ one of two styles of defense: zone or man-to-man. There are many variations within these two styles. In a zone defense, each player defends a certain area of the field. In man-to-man, each defender covers, or marks, an offensive player closely, trying to prevent him or her from getting the ball. The sweeper, a type of center-back, is often the cornerstone of the defensive unit. The sweeper usually plays closest to the goalie and is on the lookout for any balls that manage to get past the other defenders. His job is to "sweep" these balls away from the goal.

If the ball manages to get past the defenders, the task of preventing the opposite team from scoring lies on the goalkeeper alone.

The defenders and goalkeeper work with each other to form an impenetrable defense. The goalie may call out suggestions or alert a defender to an oncoming player. If a defender gains possession of the ball, he or she may pass it back to the keeper. In the past, the keeper could pick up a backward pass with his or her hands. But some players and fans felt that keepers held the ball too long. The rules were changed to speed up the game, and now the keeper must clear a backward pass with a kick.

Midfielders

Midfield players often help out both defensive and offensive teammates in a pinch. Also called halfbacks, midfielders serve as the first line of defense against the attacking team. In addition, midfielders set up offensive attacks with crisp passes to the front lines. Teams often use three midfielders: one in the middle and one on each side of the field. Great midfielders are well-rounded players who have a knack for making accurate passes.

Though Cristiano Ronaldo can play as a center forward or a striker, his favorite position is that of a center midfielder.

Attackers

The task of staying near the front lines and scoring rests with offensive specialists called the attackers. Teams usually spread three or four attackers across the field to make themselves difficult to defend. One or two center forwards (called strikers) anchor the middle of the field, while wing players attack from the sides. The striker is a team's main offensive threat. During play, the striker is most often found near the opponent's goal, covered closely by the defense. When receiving a pass, the striker must be able to control the ball quickly, evade defensive pressure, and unleash a shot on goal.

Soccer Equipment

Compared to a sport such as U.S. football, soccer requires very little equipment. But each piece serves an important purpose. Here's a look at soccer equipment from the ground up.

Footwear

Since feet and legs do most of the work in soccer, it makes sense that they have the most equipment. Players must wear cleats, shin guards, and socks. Cleats are the shoes that every player must wear. The bottoms of the shoes are covered with small cleats, or knobs, that provide traction in all playing conditions. Most cleats have hard rubber soles and a leather upper.

Since most of the action in soccer is concentrated around the feet and legs, it is important to protect them while playing. Playing without protective gear can lead to severe injury.

Shin guards are the only piece of required safety gear. They cover the front of the leg from the ankle to just below the knee. Some shin guards are made of hard, molded-plastic strips inserted into a stiff cloth backing to protect the leg. Other models are designed with a single piece of hard plastic formed around a backing of foam. The shin guards are kept in place with the help of extra-long socks.

Lionel Messi , an Argentinian player, is one of the top scorers in the world. He is the only player to gain the highest score in four consecutive Champions League Campaigns.

Shirts and Shorts

The same-colored jersey is worn by all the team members. (Goalies, however, wear a different-colored jersey for easier identification.) Each team in a league has a different color jersey. Every player has his or her own number displayed prominently on the back of the shirt.

Soccer shorts are made of lightweight material such as nylon. Heavy fabrics would restrict leg movement and absorb sweat, two things that would only slow a player down.

The entire team is dressed in the same colored shirt and shorts, except for the goalie. The English team Arsenal (shown above) wears a red and white jersey.

Goalie's Attire

The goalkeeper must be prepared to dive to the ground at any time to defend against a shot. For this reason, goalies often wear long-sleeved shirts with padding in the elbows. Long shorts with padding along the hips are also common. Additionally, padded gloves help protect many goalies' hands and help them get a better grip on the ball.

Iker Casillas (in yellow) plays as Real Madrid's goalkeeper.

Coaches

Throughout the season, most soccer teams employ one or two coaches who guide the players.

A coach helps a player in all areas of his or her game. For practices, coaches design and conduct drills and exercises that will help players improve their ball control, shot placement, and game-time decision-making. The coach is also responsible for substituting players, determining the game strategy, and assigning positions to each player.

The head coach of the Chile National team, Marcelo Bielsa, looks on during friendly game against Ukraine on September 7, 2010 in Kyiv, Ukraine.

Soccer = *Foot*ball

The foot is a valuable tool in soccer. Each part of the foot is best used for a specific purpose.

Instep: Controlling the ball, dribbling, and passing.

Outside: Turning, dribbling, and passing the ball to the side.

Top (shoelaces): Best for kicking and shooting.

Heel: Use sparingly for quick backward passes.

Sole (bottom): Use sparingly for trapping or trick moves.

Toes: Least amount of ball control. Try to avoid using your toes.

CHAPTER 3

Playing the Game

The Sun has risen, the field is marked, and the match is about to begin! The players are dressed for the game and have discussed their game strategy with the coaches. The referee blows a whistle, letting everyone know that it's time to play.

The Game Begins

Every soccer game begins with a coin toss at the center of the field. The team that wins the toss either gets possession of the ball first, or gets to choose which side of the field to defend in the first half.

Referee Igor Kruk tosses a coin during a match between FC Dynamo and FC Gomel on June 19, 2012, in Minsk, Belarus.

Eleven players from each team gather on the field. The ball is placed directly on the center line in the middle of the field. Usually, two players from the team receiving the ball first line up behind the ball. The opposing team must wait on the outside of the center circle. An official blows the whistle to signal the start of the game, and the center kicks the ball. The ball must travel one complete rotation before it is officially in play. The player who does the kickoff may not touch the ball again until another player has touched it.

Both teams try to control the ball. Any player may strike it using any part of his or her body except the hands and arms. The ball remains in play until a foul is committed or it goes out of bounds.

Goal Kicks and Corners

If the ball goes out of bounds over one of the goal lines, play is resumed with either a corner kick or a goal kick. A corner kick occurs when the defending team last touches the ball. The attacking team places the ball in the quarter-circle at the corner of the field and kicks the ball back into play. Most teams design special plays for corner kicks. Players might rush in from outside the penalty area just as the ball is kicked from the corner. These kicks are aimed precisely to one of these teammates, who can then score a goal with the help of a well-placed kick or header.

Corner kicks are great opportunities to score. With just the right amount of strategy and skill, a corner kick can very easily lead to a goal.

If the ball is kicked out of bounds over the goal line by the attacking team, then the defending team takes a goal kick from the goal area. All opposing players must vacate the penalty area. The goalie or a fullback then kicks the ball to resume play. The ball is not officially in play again until it leaves the penalty area. Some teams prefer to make short goal kicks to a midfield player nearby, while others try to kick the ball way downfield to a waiting forward.

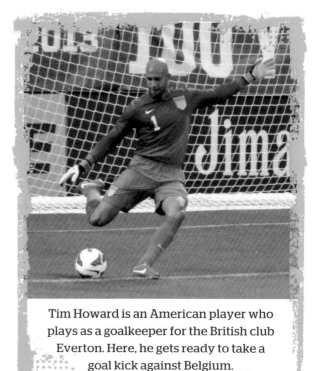

Tim Howard is an American player who plays as a goalkeeper for the British club Everton. Here, he gets ready to take a goal kick against Belgium.

The Duration

According to FIFA rules, every soccer game is ninety minutes long, divided into two forty-five-minute halves. Players get a fifteen-minute break before the second half. Since field conditions may vary, the teams switch sides of the field at the start of the second half. Many youth leagues play shorter games to accommodate the fitness level and endurance of young athletes. In leagues for younger children, the halves are usually generally thirty minutes long, while older children usually play the regulation forty-five minute halves.

If a game is tied at the end of regulation play, extra time may be needed to determine the winner. In some cases, the winner is determined by a tiebreaker or shoot-out. Each team gets five free kicks from the penalty spot, and the keeper tries to stop the shots. The team with more goals after five shots wins the game. In case the same number of goals are scored, the shoot-out continues until one team scores more than the other.

The Throw-In

The ball is declared out of bounds if it completely crosses a touchline, and the game is stopped. The team that last touched the ball loses possession, and a player from the opposing team performs a throw-in. For a regulation throw-in:

1. Locate the point where the ball went out of bounds; this will be the spot for the throw-in. Face the field. Place one hand on each side of the ball and raise the ball above your head.

2. With feet planted firmly on the ground, one in front of the other, extend your arms behind your body and prepare to throw.

3. Bring the ball forward and release with both hands at the same time. Keep both feet in contact with the ground as you release the ball. Do not step onto the field of play.

Tip:

For added power, take a running start before the throw-in. Be sure to throw at the appropriate spot and keep both feet on the ground. Plant your front foot and drag the back foot forward as you release the ball. This makes your torso generate power, thereby helping you throw the ball farther.

Running before a throw-in can increase the distance of your throw. However, it is very important to remember to throw with both hands and not to jump while throwing in order to avoid a foul.

Penalties and Referees

The referee patrols the field to ensure that no rule is being broken. In professional soccer leagues, two assistants join the referee. They determine who kicked the ball out of bounds, and they use hand signals to communicate stoppages of play.

When a referee spots a player breaking the rules, he may stop play and hold out a yellow card above the player. This serves as a warning to the player to stop the behavior. If the player commits another foul, he or she will receive a red card and be ejected from the game. Some actions, such as abusive language, fighting, or violent play, can result in an automatic red card and suspension. Substitution for the ejected player is not allowed, and the team must play with one less player for the rest of the game.

It is a referee's responsibility to suspend players who commit a serious foul. Here, Rodrigo Burgos of Paraguay (in white) is shown a yellow card during a FIFA World Cup match between Egypt and Paraguay in Cairo, Egypt in 2009.

Only the more serious fouls committed during a game get a yellow or red card. The referee stops play for other fouls as well. Play is resumed with a free kick by the team that did not commit the penalty. There are several types of free kicks:

Penalty kicks are a boon to the offense. It becomes extremely difficult for the goalkeeper to block it because he or she has no defenders to help him or her.

Indirect

Less serious offenses result in an indirect kick to resume play. The kick occurs at the site of the foul. It is not possible to score a goal on an indirect kick. The ball must first touch another player.

Direct

A direct kick is reserved for serious fouls, such as touching the ball with your hands or violent play. A goal may be scored from a direct kick. Opposing players must stand at least ten yards away when the ball is kicked. If a direct kick is near the goal, defensive players may group themselves together ten yards away to form a defensive "wall." The kicker does not get a clear view of the goal, and his chances of scoring are lower.

Penalty

When a defensive player commits a serious foul in his or her own penalty area, the opposing team is awarded a penalty kick. The ball is placed on the penalty spot, and one player is allowed to take a shot on goal. All players except the shooter and the goalie must clear out of the penalty area until the ball is kicked. It is very difficult for a goalie to stop a penalty shot. Professional goalies try to anticipate where the ball will be kicked so they can move into position. This can be difficult because skilled kickers disguise the direction of their shot until the last moment. If the goalie moves too soon, the kicker can kick the other way.

Offsides

One rule in soccer that frequently creates confusion is the offsides ruling. The penalty is intended to prevent offensive players from hanging around the opponent's goal, waiting to score. The rule states that at least two defensive players (including the keeper) must be between an offensive player and the goal when the ball is passed in the offensive player's direction.

It is important for attackers to make sure that there is at least one defender behind them when they are taking a pass.

This essentially means that an offensive player must stay in front of the defender closest to the goal before receiving a pass from a teammate.

Essential Skills

There are six essential skills that every aspiring soccer player should develop. These skills must be practiced over and over before one can become a top-notch player. It is impossible to be a "perfect player," as there are aspects of your game that can always be improved further.

Dribbling is possibly the most important skill for players to possess.

Dribbling

The art of running and changing direction while controlling the ball with your feet is called dribbling. In the beginning, you want to get used to the feel of running quickly while propelling the ball a short distance in front of you with light kicks. As you gain confidence, you'll learn how to change direction and evade defenders. To dribble past an opponent, slow down as you approach. Then, just as you reach the opponent, pass by with a sudden burst of speed and change of direction.

Try to keep the ball moving at all times. A stopped ball is more likely to be taken away by a defender. Keep your head up so you can keep an eye on the field around you. If you have to stop dribbling, keep possession of the ball by turning your back and using your body to block your opponent. Be careful not to push or hold the opposing player with your arms, which is a foul.

Passing

Accurate passing is often the secret of a team's offensive success. For a short pass, kick the ball with the inside (instep) of your foot. The instep is the largest kicking surface and gives you the greatest accuracy. To make a long pass downfield, use the top of

The player passes the ball to avoid having it taken by an opposing player, and to advance it down the field.

your foot along the shoelaces to kick the ball. It will sail through the air and reach the other side of the field. You can use the outside of your foot to make quick passes to the side. It is important to practice passing with both feet.

There are several passing strategies that can quickly penetrate the defense of an opposing team. One of the most common is the wall pass. When a defender approaches as you are dribbling the ball, pass the ball to a teammate slightly ahead of you and to the side. As the defender shifts to cover your teammate, sprint hard down the field. Your teammate can then pass the ball back to you. Your teammate serves as the "wall" that bounces your pass right back to you.

Shooting

Scoring opportunities are worthless unless they are converted into goals.

Wayne Rooney of Manchester United plays a friendly match against Malaysia in 2009.

Mastering the art of shooting with both feet takes practice and patience. As you work on your passing game, you are actually building all the skills necessary to be a great shooter: ball control, accurate ball placement, and power.

Good players can make the ball spin or curve in the air by striking it on certain spots and with different parts of their foot. When shooting, keep your arms out for balance, and keep your head over the ball. This helps the ball stay low and improves your accuracy. To evade the goalkeeper and score successfully, try aiming at the far corners of the net.

Trapping

Trapping is an important skill to possess. When a teammate passes you the ball, you have to settle the ball to the ground quickly. This often requires you to "trap" the ball with some part of your body so that it doesn't bounce out of control. Effective trapping is possible with virtually any part of the body. Experienced players can trap the ball with their legs, chest, feet, and even their backside.

To trap the ball, you must use your body to absorb the speed of the ball. As the ball reaches your foot or chest, let your body relax. If your body is tense, the ball will bounce too far from you to control it.

This player traps the ball with his chest.

Tackling

Attacking the player with the ball—tackling—is an important skill. You may knock the ball away from the front, back, or side as your opponent dribbles it. Some players even dive and slide to knock the ball away. If it seems like you are using your body to knock the other player

Tackling is an important skill required to gain control of the ball.

down or off balance, instead of attempting to pursue the ball, the referee will call a foul. Especially when attempting a slide tackle, make sure that you touch the ball before making contact with any part of your opponent's body. If you strike your opponent's body first, you will be called for a foul.

Players fight for the ball during the Champions league match between Liverpool and Real Madrid on February 25, 2009 in Madrid.

Headers

In soccer, your head is another tool you can use for controlling the ball. With practice, you can turn your head just as you make contact with the ball, sending it in any direction you want. A simple practice drill can improve your headers. Stand a few feet from a teammate and have him or her gently throw the ball in the air toward you. Return the ball by striking it with your forehead. To expand your header skills, you can ask your teammate to move to the side or stand farther behind.

Headers can be useful to score goals. Aaron Ramsey, an Arsenal player, scores a goal against Malaysia using a header on July 13, 2011.

CHAPTER 4

Getting Involved

To perform well on the field, soccer players must be in excellent shape. In the early weeks of a season, it is common to see players with their hands on their knees, trying to catch their breath.

Maintaining Fitness

It is important to stay in shape before the season begins. There are many fun ways to train the muscles that you will use in a soccer game. Riding a bike is great for building strong legs and endurance. Swimming provides a full-body workout and improves lung capacity. You should exercise your body at least three times a week.

Playing soccer requires you to be in shape since it demands a lot of stamina.
Cycling and stretching are good ways to exercise your muscles.

In addition to getting enough exercise, it is important to eat a balanced diet. Try to avoid processed foods such as candy and soda. The high sugar content doesn't give your body the consistent energy it needs. Complex carbohydrates, such as pasta, are a great choice for dinner the night before a game. Breads and pastas are easily broken down by your muscles into usable energy. Get to bed early, too. While you sleep, your body repairs itself and gets ready for the next big game.

Warming Up, Cooling Down

Once the whistle blows to start the game, you can go from a standstill to a full run in a matter of seconds. If your muscles aren't ready, you have a much higher risk of injury. Before a game, players usually warm up their bodies with light running, stretching, and some passing and shooting drills. Try to complete this diligently, and don't forget to stretch before you step onto the field.

School players warming up before playing in an effort to avoid injuries.

If you don't have enough time for a full routine, make sure all the major muscles in your legs are warmed up. Quadriceps are the powerful muscles that run from your knees to your hip and provide your kicking and acceleration power. Your hamstrings cover the back side of your upper leg and must be stretched to maintain balance between muscle groups. Your calf muscles run from the heel to the back of the knee and help push off from the ground when running.

When the game ends, be sure to give your body some time to cool down before you stop moving. Walk slowly around the field until your heart rate returns to normal. To avoid a sore body, cool down and drink plenty of fluids.

Leg Stretches

- **Quadriceps:** Stand upright on both feet. Bend one leg behind you, raising your foot to your buttock. Using the hand on the same side of your body, gently pull your foot closer to the buttock. Feel the stretch in the front of your leg.

Stretching the quadriceps helps prepare and loosen up the thighs. The leg that you're standing on should be slightly bent.

- **Hamstrings:** Stand upright on both feet. Keeping your back straight, slowly bend forward and let your arms dangle. You will feel a stretch in the back of your legs. Don't bounce.

Touching your toes is a great way to stretch your hamstrings and back muscles.

- **Calves:** Stand with both your feet on a stair, or some other slightly elevated surface. Place the toes of one foot on the edge of the stair and slowly let your body weight extend your heel downward. You will feel a stretch in the calf muscles.

Exercising the calves before a game is very important.

Injuries

By warming up and cooling down faithfully, you may be able to avoid one of soccer's most common injuries—the muscle cramp. A muscle cramp occurs when one or more muscles contract powerfully and stay that way. Cramps can be quite painful. It usually helps to gently stretch out the muscle that is cramping. The good news about cramps is that they don't last long.

Hamstring injuries are one of the most common soccer-related injuries.

Many rules in soccer are designed to avoid injuries. For instance, players are not allowed to kick the ball near another player's head. Also, sliding into an opponent's legs is forbidden. These rules help maintain the safety of the sport. But with every sport, injuries do occur. The most vulnerable parts of the soccer athlete's body are the knees and ankles. The legs take a lot of abuse in a full-speed game of soccer. The ligaments and tendons that hold your knees and ankles together can be stretched if you fall or twist in an awkward way. If you have injured yourself in the past, it is always wise to use extra protection during games. A soft brace is a useful buy if you want to stabilize a weakened knee or ankle.

Buying Equipment

It is not very difficult to go out and buy equipment once you've decided that you want to play soccer. A ball is all that's really needed to play with friends in your neighborhood. When joining a team, you'll need to buy cleats, socks, shorts, and shin guards. You can usually find all these things at your local sporting goods store. Cleats are the most expensive item and, in many ways, the most important. Take your time when selecting cleats. Most teams supply the official jersey for you to wear, so don't worry about buying one.

Youth Leagues

Getting started on a team is pretty easy. Among young people, soccer is one of the most popular sports, and youth leagues are generously sprinkled all throughout North America.

Youth leagues are very common. Children enjoying a game of soccer
at the Cypress Park, Coral Springs.

There are many large organizations that monitor league activities. There are also many local independent leagues to choose from. Most leagues have teams for players from the ages of five to eighteen. Both boys and girls are invited to play. Some leagues mix boys and girls together on the same teams (called "coed" teams), while others maintain a separate league for each.

A soccer season usually lasts for about three months. Many leagues organize one season in the spring and another in the fall. A common spring schedule is March through May, and a fall season may run from September through November. During the season, you will probably practice with your team once during the week and then play a game on the weekend. Be prepared for a range of temperatures. A spring season that starts with frosty grass in March can end with scorching sun in late May.

Soccer camps are a great way to improve your skills and stay in shape during the summer months. It's fun to meet other players, too. Camps usually last one or two weeks. Experienced instructors spend hours each day honing every aspect of your game.

Many high schools assemble their own soccer teams to compete against other school teams. Coaches hold tryouts to select the best players. Those who are exceptionally skilled may go on to play competitive soccer at the college level or even the professional level. For the rest of us, colleges and universities generally have intramural programs, which are mini-leagues that are open to all students. There are opportunities to play team soccer well into your adult life, as municipal adult leagues are common in most areas.

It's Not Only About Winning

Soccer, like any sport, can be highly competitive. Some athletes dedicate their lives to it and want to win at all costs. But a majority of athletes just play for the love of the game. If you enjoy soccer but don't expect to be the next David Beckham or Ronaldinho, don't worry. It's all about letting go and enjoying yourself.

Glossary

center forward A player who is positioned in the middle of the field on offense.

cleats Sports shoes that have hard rubber spikes attached to the underside to provide traction.

corner kick A direct free kick from a corner of the field. It is awarded to the attacking team when the ball has been driven out of bounds over the goal line by a defender.

FC Short for football club. The clubs of English Premier League (EPL) are usually followed by FC.

fullback A primarily defensive backfield player whose position is near the defensive goal.

goal kick A free kick that is awarded to a defensive team when an opponent has driven the ball out of bounds over the goal line.

halfback One of several players stationed behind the forward line of attacking players. Also referred to as being a midfielder.

hexagon A six sided shape in which all the sides are of an equal length.

instep The arched middle part of the foot between the toes and the ankle.

ligament The fibrous tissue that connects one bone to another.

offsides Illegally ahead of the ball in the attacking zone.

tendon A tough tissue that connects the muscle to the bone.

throw-in A way to restart play after the ball has gone out of bounds.

touchline Either of the sidelines bordering the playing field.

rugby A game similar to American football. The ball may be kicked, carried, and passed from hand to hand.

wing Either of the forward positions played near the sideline.

For More Information

American Youth Soccer Organization
12501 S. Isis Avenue
Hawthorne, CA 90250
(800) 872-2976
Web site: http://www.ayso.org

National Soccer Hall of Fame
18 Stadium Circle
Oneonta, NY 13820
(607) 432-3351
Web site: http://www.soccerhall.org

United Soccer Leagues
1715 N. Westshore Blvd., Suite 825
Tampa FL 33607
(813) 963-3909
Web site: http://www.uslsoccer.com

U.S. Adult Soccer Association
7000 S. Harlem Ave
Bridgeview, IL 60455
(708) 496-6870
Web site: http://www.usasa.com

U.S. Soccer Association
1801 S. Prairie Avenue
Chicago, IL 60616
(312) 808-1300
Web site: http://www.ussoccer.com

U.S. Soccer Foundation
1211 Connecticut Avenue, NW Suite 500
Washington, DC 20036
(202) 872-9277
Web site: http://www.ussoccerfoundation.org

U.S. Youth Soccer Association
899 Presidential Drive, Suite 117
Richardson, TX 75081
(972) 235-4499
Web site: http://www.usyouthsoccer.org

Web Sites

Due to the changing nature of Internet links, Rosen Publishing has developed
an online list of web sites related to the subject of this book. This site is updated
regularly. Please use this link to access the list:

http://www.rosenlinks.com/STTS/Socc

For Further Reading

Aczel, German. *The World Cup 1930-2010*. London, UK: Sportsbooks, 2010.

Angelo Lisi, Clemente. *The U.S. Women's Soccer Team: An American Success Story*. New York, NY: Taylor Trade Publishing, 2013.

Barnes, Stuart. *Nationwide Annual 2012-13: Soccer's pocket Encyclopedia*. London, UK: Sportsbooks, 2012.

Beale, Michael. *Soccer Academy: 100 Defending Practices and Small Sided Games*. New York, NY: Reedswain Incorporated, 2008.

Fared, Grant. *Long Distance Love: A Passion for Football*. Philadelphia, PA: Temple University Press, U.S., 2008.

Kuhn, Gabriel. *Soccer Vs. The State*. Oakland, CA: PM Press, 2011.

Kuper, Simon. *Soccernomics*. London, UK: HarperSport, 2012.

Marquez, Ryan. *Beautiful Soccer: Creating Passion & Confidence in Young Players*. Chula Vista, CA: Tracks Publishing, 2012.

Rhody, Ron; Rhody, Chris. *SOCCER: A Spectator's Guide*. New York, NY: Academy Publishing, 2010.

Torres, Fernando. *Torres: El Niño: My Story*. London, UK: HarperSport, 2009.

Bibliography

Brandbeat. "Soccer: A Global Game With National Appeal."
March 10, 2005. Retrieved April 10, 2006
(http://www.brandbeat.com/brandbeat/?m=200503).

Crisfield, D. W. *The Complete Idiot's Guide to Soccer*.
New York, NY: Alpha Books, 1999.

Decatur Sports. "U.S. Soccer Participation Steady at 18.2 Million."
April 17, 1998. Retrieved April 7, 2006 (http://www.decatursports.com/
articles/soccer_participation.htm).

Gifford, Clive. *Soccer: The Ultimate Guide to the Beautiful
Game*. New York, NY: Kingfisher Publications, 2002.

Harvey, Gill, et al. *The Usborne Complete Soccer School*.
London, UK: Usborne Publishing, 1998.

Ominsky, Dave, and P. J. Harari. *Soccer Made Simple:
A Spectator's Guide*. Los Angeles, CA: First Base Sports, Inc., 1994.

Ramsay, Graham. *Soccer for Girls: An Introductory Step-by-Step Guide*.
London, UK: Carlton Books, 1998.

Index

A

attackers, 16, 18

C

camps, soccer, 41
cleats, 18, 40
coach, role of, 22
corner kick, 13, 15, 25

D

defenders, 16-17, 30, 31, 32

E

equipment, 10, 18, 20, 40

F

Fédération Internationale de Football
    Association (FIFA), 6-7, 8, 14, 26
field, soccer, 12-13
fitness, player, 36-41
fouls, 25, 28-30, 31, 34
free kicks, 26, 29

G

game basics, 13, 15-18, 24-25, 27-34
goalie/goalkeeper, 12, 13, 15, 16, 17, 20,
    26, 30, 32

H

headers, 25, 34
history of soccer 4-8, 11

I

injuries, 39

M

Major League Soccer (MLS), 11
midfielders, 17

N

North American Soccer League
    (NASL), 10

O

offsides, 30

P

Pelé, 10
penalties, 28-30
positions, player, 15-18

R

red card, 28, 29
referees, 28
rules, 5-6, 14, 17, 26, 28, 30, 39

S

shin guards, 18, 40
shoot-out, 8, 26
skills, essential playing, 30-34
stretching, 37-39
striker, 18

T

throw-in, 27

U

United States Soccer Federation, 11, 12

W

World Cup, 6-8, 10, 11, 14
    women in, 8

Y

yellow card, 28
youth leagues, 11, 14, 26, 40-41

About the Authors

Jeremy Cooperson is a writer based in the Washington D.C. metropolitan area. He is a proud soccer dad who enjoys cheering on his children's teams.

Growing up in North Carolina, Brian Wingate spent many seasons on the soccer field. He played amateur soccer from age ten through high school. During his time at the University of North Carolina-Chapel Hill, Wingate played intramural collegiate soccer and coached a youth soccer team. Besides his playing experience, Wingate has served as a youth league referee.

Photo Credits